Starting with...
Role play

At the garage/
At the airport

Diana Bentley

Maggie Hutchings

Dee Reid

Diana Bentley is an educational consultant for primary literacy and has written extensively for both teachers and children. She worked for many years in the Centre for the Teaching of Reading at Reading University and then became a Senior Lecturer in Primary English at Oxford Brookes University. Throughout her professional life she has continued to work in schools and teach children aged from 5 to 11 years.

Maggie Hutchings has considerable experience teaching KS1 and Early Years. She is a Leading Teacher for literacy in The Foundation Stage and is a Foundation Stage and Art coordinator. Maggie is passionate about the importance of learning through play and that learning should be an exciting and fun experience for young children. Her school's art work has been exhibited in The National Gallery, London.

Dee Reid is a former teacher who has been an independent consultant in primary literacy for over 20 years in many local authorities. She is consultant to 'Catch Up' – a special needs literacy intervention programme used in over 4,000 schools in the UK. She is Series Consultant to 'Storyworlds' (Heinemann) and her recent publications include 'Think About It' (Nelson Thornes) and Literacy World (Heinemann).

Other titles in the series:

Colour and light
Under the ground
Emergency 999
Into space
At the shops
Fairytales
At the hospital
All creatures great and small
On the farm
Water
Ourselves

Other Foundation titles:

Starting with stories and poems:

Self esteem
Self care
A sense of community
Making relationships
Behaviour and self control

A collection of stories and poems

Starting with our bodies and movement

Starting with sounds and letters

The authors would like to thank Jane Whitwell for all her hard work in compiling the resources and poems for the series.

Published by
Hopscotch Educational Publishing Ltd, Unit 2, The Old Brushworks, 56 Pickwick Road, Corsham, Wiltshire, SN13 9BX Tel: 01249 701701

© 2006 Hopscotch Educational Publishing

Written by Diana Bentley, Maggie Hutchings and Dee Reid
Series design by Blade Communications
Cover illustration by Sami Sweeten
Illustrated by Kirsty Wilson
Printed by Colorman (Ireland) Ltd

ISBN 1 905390 18 1

Diana Bentley, Maggie Hutchings and Dee Reid hereby assert their moral right to be identified as the authors of this work in accordance with the Copyright, Designs and Patents Act, 1988.

The authors and publisher would like to thank Chapter One (a specialist children's bookshop) in Wokingham for all their help and support. Email: chapteronebookshop@yahoo.co.uk

Contents

Acknowledgements

The authors and publisher gratefully acknowledge permission to reproduce copyright material in this book.

'Gran's van' by Cynthia Rider from *The Oxford Phonic Kit Pack 2*, Oxford University Press (2002). © Cynthia Rider. Reproduced by kind permission of the author.
'My bike' by John Kitching from *Twinkle, twinkle chocolate bar*, compiled by John Foster, Oxford University Press. © John Kitching. Reproduced by kind permission of the author.
'Looping the loop' by Charles Thomson from *Early Years Poems and Rhymes Collections* compiled by Jill Bennett, Scholastic. © Charles Thomson. Reproduced by kind permission of the author.
'Aeroplanes, aeroplanes' by Barbara Ireson from *Early Years Poems and Rhymes Collections* compiled by Jill Bennett, Scholastic. © Barbara Ireson. Reproduced by kind permission of the author.

Every effort has been made to trace the owners of copyright of material in this book and the publisher apologises for any inadvertent omissions. Any persons claiming copyright for any material should contact the publisher who will be happy to pay the permission fees agreed between them and who will amend the information in this book on any subsequent reprint.

Introduction

There are 12 books in the series **Starting with role play** offering a complete curriculum for the Early Years.

Ourselves	At the garage/At the airport
Into space	Emergency 999
At the shops	All creatures great and small
Colour and light	Under the ground
At the hospital	Fairytales
On the farm	Water

While each topic is presented as a six-week unit of work, it can easily be adapted to run for fewer weeks if necessary. The themes have been carefully selected to appeal to boys and girls and to a range of cultural groups.

 Each unit addresses all six areas of learning outlined in the *Curriculum Guidance for the Foundation Stage* and the specific Early Learning Goal is identified for each activity and indicated by this symbol.

Generally, differentiation is achieved by outcome, although for some of the Communication, Language and Literacy strands and Mathematical Development strands, extension activities are suggested for older or more confident learners.

Suggested teaching sequence for each unit

Each week has been organised into a suggested teaching sequence. However, each activity in an area of learning links to other activities and there will be overlap as groups engage with the tasks.

The Core Curriculum: Literacy and Mathematics

Every school will have its own programmes for literacy and mathematics and it is not intended that the activities in the units in this book should replace these. Rather, the activities suggested aim to support any programme, to help to consolidate the learning and to demonstrate how the learning can be used in practical situations.

The importance of role play

'Children try out their most recent learning, skills and competences when they play. They seem to celebrate what they know.'

Tina Bruce (2001) Learning Through Play: Babies, Toddlers and the Foundation Years. London: Hodder & Stoughton.

Early Years practitioners are aware of the importance of play as a vehicle for learning. When this play is carefully structured and managed then the learning opportunities are greatly increased. Adult participation can be the catalyst for children's imaginations and creativity.

Six weeks allows for a role play area to be created, developed and expanded and is the optimum time for inspiring children and holding their interest. It is important not to be too prescriptive in the role play area. Teachers should allow for children's ideas and interests to evolve and allow time for the children to explore and absorb information. Sometimes, the children will take the topic off at a tangent or go into much greater depth than expected or even imagined.

Organising the classroom

The role play area could be created by partitioning off a corner of the classroom with ceiling drapes, an old-style clothes-horse, chairs, boxes, large-scale construction blocks (for example, 'Quadro') or even an open-fronted beach tent/shelter. Alternatively, the whole classroom could be dedicated to the role play theme.

Involving parents and carers

Encourage the children to talk about the topic and what they are learning with their parents or carers at home. With adult help and supervision, they can explore the internet and search for pictures in magazines and books. This enriches the learning taking place in the classroom.

Outside activities

The outdoor classroom should be an extension of the indoor classroom and it should support and enhance the activities offered inside. Boys, in particular, often feel less restricted in outdoor play. They may use language more purposefully and may even engage more willingly in reading and writing activities. In the outdoor area things can be done on a much bigger, bolder and noisier scale and this may connect with boys' preferred learning styles.

Observation in Salford schools and settings noted that boys access books much more readily when there is a book area outdoors.

Resources

Role play areas can be more convincing reconstructions when they are stocked with authentic items. Car boot sales, jumble sales and charity shops are good sources of artefacts. It is a good idea to inform parents and carers of topics well in advance so they can be looking out for objects and materials that will enhance the role play area.

Reading

Every week there should be a range of opportunities for children to participate in reading experiences. These should include:

Shared reading

The practitioner should read aloud to the children from Big Books, modelling the reading process; for example, demonstrating that print is read from left to right. Shared reading also enables the practitioner to draw attention to high frequency words, the spelling patterns of different words and punctuation. Where appropriate, the practitioner should cover words and ask the children to guess which word would make sense in the context. This could also link with phonic work where the children could predict the word based on seeing the initial phoneme. Multiple readings of the same text enable them to become familiar with story language and tune in to the way written language is organised into sentences.

Independent reading

As children become more confident with the written word they should be encouraged to recognise high frequency words. Practitioners should draw attention to these words during shared reading and shared writing. Children should have the opportunity to read these words in context and to play word matching and word recognition games. Encourage the children to use their ability to hear the sounds at various points in words and to use their knowledge of those phonemes to decode simple words.

Writing

Shared writing

Writing opportunities should include teacher demonstration, teacher scribing, copy writing and independent writing. (Suggestions for incorporating shared writing are given each week.)

Emergent writing

The role play area should provide ample opportunities for children to write purposefully, linking their writing with the task in hand. These meaningful writing opportunities help children to understand more about the writing process and to seek to communicate in writing. Children's emergent writing should occur alongside their increasing awareness of the 'correct' form of spellings. In the example below, the child is beginning to have an understanding of letter shapes as well as the need to write from left to right.

Assessment

When children are actively engaged in the role play area this offers ample opportunities for practitioners to undertake observational assessments. By participating in the role play area the practitioner can take time to talk in role to the children about their work and assess their performance. The assessment grid on page 39 enables practitioners to record progress through the appropriate Stepping Stone or Early Learning Goal.

DfES publications

The following publications will be useful:

Progression in Phonics (DfES 0178/2000)
Developing Early Writing (DfES 0055/2001)
Playing with Sounds (DfES 0280/2004)

At the garage/airport	Role play area	Personal, Social and Emotional Development	Communication, Language and Literacy	Knowledge and Understanding of the World	Mathematical Development	Creative Development	Physical Development
Week 1	Setting up the garage	*Speak in familiar group* Talking about taking turns	*Extend their vocabulary* Making labels, name cards and class book	*Find out about objects* Discussing the function of a garage	*Use ideas to solve problems* Sorting tools by shape and purpose Making graphs of different cars	*Use a wide range of materials* Making the garage, petrol pumps and job sheets	*Move with control and coordination* Construction kits Experimenting with tools
Week 2	Making collage of wheels Servicing cars	*Initiate ideas* Talking about inventions	*Retell narrative in correct sequence* Reading story and asking class to retell it	*Look at similarities and changes* Experimenting with wheels	*Add and subtract* Using wheels for adding and subtracting	*Use imagination in art* Printing with wheels and wheel collage	*Use range of large and small equipment* Ball games and hoops
Week 3	Adapting garage into a showroom	*Form good relations with adults and peers* Meeting and greeting customers	*Listen with enjoyment and respond to stories* Sharing fiction and non-fiction books about cars	*Look at differences and change* Experimenting with rusting nails	*Use IT in problem solving* Programming Roamer to move	*Use imagination in design* Designing cars and showroom	*Move with control* Moving in various ways as a car Playing racing cars
Week 4	Changing role play area into airport	*Treat people with respect* Talking about jobs in airport and treating all people with courtesy and respect	*Use talk to organise, sequence and clarify thinking* Discussing questions for passengers Making passports	*Ask questions about why things happen* Discussing airports and journeys	*Use language to compare quantities* Weighing and estimating	*Explore colour and texture in different dimensions* Creating background for airport Making check-in desk	*Recognise changes in their body when active* Moving with different objects and weights Discussing how you feel
Week 5	Making model of airport and aeroplanes	*Consider consequences of actions* Discussing tidying up	*Use language to recreate roles* Recording announcements Playing phoneme frames	*Identify uses of technology* Using a tape recorder for making airport announcements	*Recreate simple map jigsaws* Sequencing runway lights Counting aircraft	*Communicate ideas using range of materials* Making pop-up airport Making paper planes	*Show awareness of space* Following signs and symbols Following oral instructions
Week 6	Making the inside of an aircraft	*Show range of feelings* Talking about greeting people and saying goodbye	*Know that print carries meaning* Writing postcards	*Know own culture and those of other people* Talking about other cultures and being in another country	*Recognise patterns in numbers* Estimating space in aircraft Counting passengers	*Use imagination in art and design* In-flight catering Creating an in-flight meal	*Handle objects with control* Mirroring movements Pouring water while moving

At the garage

During this six-week unit, the children will investigate work and workers at the garage and the airport. The unit is divided into two three-week topics. The cross-curricular activities will include exploration of wheels and transport, tools and equipment, and going on a journey.

If possible, invite a car mechanic or someone who works in a garage to come and talk to the children. (For Week 3 invite a sales representative to come to the class.)

At the end of the unit, as well as contributing to the role play area, the children will have:
- made a garage
- created a collage
- written advertisements
- designed a car
- used a digital camera
- made passports
- made paper aeroplanes
- made in-flight food for passengers

WEEK 1

The role play area

During this week the children will set up the garage. They will make **cupboards**, **petrol pumps** and a **car-wash** and create **jobs sheets**. They will talk about the functions of a garage, the people who work in it and the tools used. They will learn about vehicles, name main car parts and, through role play, develop their communication skills.

Setting up the garage

Resources

Photocopiable:

Poems and songs 1 (page 31)

Fiction books:

The Helpful Mechanic by Margaret Eustace, 'Little Stories' series, Ladybird (0 721419 94 1)
Mr Gumpy's Motor Car by John Burningham, Red Fox (0 099417 95 2)

Non-fiction books:

Ben's Big Book of Cars by Ben Blathwayt, Red Fox (0 099404 72 9)
Cars, Trucks and Things That Go by Richard Scarry, Harper Collins (0 007111 44 4)

Materials:

- Children's toolkits
- Inner tubes from bicycles
- Funnels
- Large milk container
- Plastic jugs
- Small pots or containers
- Plastic tubes or piping
- Car jack (a real one for investigation)
- Buckets, sponges and rags
- Hubcaps
- Small tyres (real and toy)
- Construction kits, such as Mobilo and Plastic Meccano
- Large boxes
- Till
- Selection of toy cars and other vehicles
- Small boxes ('Cuppa Soup' size)
- Pompoms (as used by cheerleaders)
- Two small bags of sand

Knowledge and Understanding of the World

 Find out about objects they observe.

Introducing the topic

- ❑ Hold a class discussion: What do we know about cars and garages? Ask the children if they have ever visited a garage with an adult. Do they know anyone who works in a garage? What did they see in the garage? Do all garages sell petrol? Do all garages have a car-wash? Do all garages sell cars? What else do they sell? Make a list of the different functions of a garage.

- ❑ Take groups of children into the school car park, when it is safe to do so, to look at parts of a car. Where is the engine? Look under the bonnet, if possible, and open up the boot.

- ❑ Look at and talk about tools and their purpose. Think about how mechanics can work underneath vehicles. Talk about inspection ramps. Ask: What makes a car move? How does the driver make the car turn? How do you know when a car is going to turn? How does a car stop? Where is the petrol stored in the car? Talk about headlamps and fog lights, day and night driving, and safety. What happens if you break down on the road? Talk about recovery vehicles, how to keep safe in a car, wearing a seatbelt and car seats for young children.

Creative Development

 Express and communicate their ideas, thoughts and feelings by using a wide range of materials.

Creating the background

- ❑ On large sheets of paper (possibly fawn coloured sugar paper or brown parcel paper), print brick or stone patterns with foam or sponge blocks.

Adding features

- ❑ Build doors and cupboards. Cupboards could be made out of boxes and pinned to the background. Label each piece of equipment (see Communication, Language and Literacy). Add authentic materials to the area, such as an inner tube from a bicycle, hubcaps, small tyres, a car jack and toy toolkits.

- ❑ Place a table in the role play area for the reception desk and paint large boxes for use as workbenches. Add a notice board and telephone.

- ❑ Make petrol pumps out of boxes and lengths of hose or flexible piping. Place these in the role play area. Encourage the children to fill their tank and then pay. Make signs showing the petrol price.

- ❑ Create some job sheets (see below and at the top of the next page). Turn five small boxes (Cuppa Soup size) inside out, reassemble them and ask the children to paint them. Cut the tops off. Make

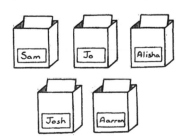

cards, cut just longer than the boxes. On each card draw a different job; for example, a flat tyre, a broken exhaust, a leaking radiator, a car-wash attendant and a receptionist and label them. Place the cards in the boxes for the children to select their job. They should stick their name card (see Communication, Language and Literacy) onto the front of the box to indicate the job they are working on.

Flat tyre   Broken exhaust   Receptionist

Leaking radiator   Car wash attendant

Outside

Creating a car-wash

❑ Provide buckets of water, sponges and rags for the children to use to wash vehicles. Make or buy pompoms and fix them to the sides of two boxes. Place the boxes so that the children can drive their vehicles between them. (Place a bag of sand inside each box to prevent them moving too much.)

❑ Talk about what would happen if you were using a real car-wash and you forgot to close the windows!

Personal, Social and Emotional Development

 Be confident to try new activities, initiate ideas and speak in a familiar group.

Circle time

❑ Talk about how important it is to take turns and to respect each other's ideas. Decide on the roles in the garage and discuss how to ensure that everyone has a turn and how they will know who is in what role.

❑ Take it in turns to describe a journey. For example, 'My mummy took me to see my grandma. We went by car and it was a long way. We had to stop at a garage to put some petrol in the car. I was glad when we got to Grandma's.'

Mathematical Development

 Use developing mathematical ideas and methods to solve practical problems.

Counting – days of the week

❑ Practise saying the days of the week. Talk about which days your garage will be open. Ask: How many days will your garage be open during the week? How many days will it be closed?

Sorting

❑ Look at the collection of tools. Sort them by shape and purpose – for example, tools used for cutting, tools used for tightening, sharp tools and heavy tools. Take opportunities to talk about care when handling potentially dangerous tools.

Number work

❑ Make a list of prices for the garage. For example, Servicing – £10 and MOT – £5 (prices may not be realistic but this is an opportunity for more able children to work with £s and larger numbers).

Data collection and simple block graphs

❑ Draw a simple outline of a car and photocopy it onto thin card for each child. Ask them to colour it the colour of their family car (or one they would like) and cut it out. Glue them all onto a piece of card that has been prepared as a grid with colours along the bottom. When complete, discuss the graph. Which is the most popular colour? Talk about how we can use graphs to show our findings.

Extension

❑ Encourage the more able children to make a similar graph but to show how the children get to school – by foot, by car or by public transport.

Outside

❑ Take groups of children into the school car park to look at the cars – shapes, colours, labels or emblems. Ask: How many wheels does a car have? What shape are the wheels? Can you see any other circles? What shape are the windows? If there are four cars parked in a line, how many wheels are there altogether?

Communication, Language and Literacy

 Extend their vocabulary, exploring the meanings and sounds of new words.

Listening

❑ Read a story about a car (see Resources). Read it through several times and then invite the children to join in with you as you read. Encourage them to act out the story in the role play area, using the vocabulary of the book.

Writing: teacher scribing – labels

❑ Scribe labels for the children to copy, such as the name of the garage, Service Centre (on a door), Spares, Repairs, To the Car-wash, Enquiries and Reception.

❑ Ask the children to help you label parts of the car. Have ready a large picture or poster of a car. Scribe onto small pieces of card and ask the children to place the labels appropriately, using sticky tack. (See Knowledge and Understanding of the World: car park visit.)

Independent writing

❑ Support the children as they make name cards for the job sheets (see Creative Development). For less confident children, write their names in highlighter pen and ask them to go over the letters in pencil. Other children could copy from a teacher's model or write independently. Laminate the name cards and store in the garage.

Extension

❑ Give each child one of the photocopies of the car (see Mathematical Development). Ask them to write three sentences about it; for example, 'This car is blue. It has four doors. It goes fast.'

Making a class book

❑ Make a book with the title 'Oh! No! My car won't go!' Each child draws their car. Maybe it has a flat tyre, has crashed, has run out of fuel or won't start. They draw themselves next to the car. Ask: Do you look happy or sad? Has anyone come to help you?

❑ Help them to write a simple sentence underneath the picture – for example, 'My car won't go.' (A simple way of making these sheets into a book is to use a slip-in presentation folder.)

❑ Use this book for discussion with groups. Ask: Can you see why James' car won't go? What do you think he should do?

Observing signs

❑ Encourage the children, with parental help, to list some petrol companies. How many can they find? Esso, Shell, Total and so on. They could write them down and bring them in for display.

Song

❑ Sing 'Garage mechanic's song' (page 31).

Physical Development

 Move with control and coordination. Handle tools, objects and construction materials safely and with increasing control.

Movement

❑ Think about the observations made when sorting tools (see Mathematical Development). Explore movement – for example, a screwdriver twists in a jerky fashion one way to tighten and the other way to loosen. It becomes more difficult to turn as it tightens. Pretend you are levering something heavy. Show how strong you are. Pretend you are driving a car. Turn your head and the steering wheel as you move to all the spaces in the room or playground.

Working with construction kits

❑ Ask the children to build a vehicle with wheels that turn. What tools will they use? Are they difficult to use? Are they twisting them, turning them or using them to hammer?

WEEK 2

The role play area

During this week the children will make a **collage** of different wheels, and thread and sew different **circular cards**. They will each illustrate and write part of a story to display on the classroom wall.

In the role play area they will continue to service the cars and deal with customers. They will wash the cars and sell petrol.

The children will also learn about invention and why 'wheels' are so useful and important in our lives.

collage
threading cards
Job Sheet
Tool Box
petrol pump
car-wash

Resources

Photocopiable:

Poems and songs (page 31)

Fiction books:

Bruno and the Old Car by Colin and Jacqui Hawkins, Orchard Books (1 843624 12 5)
Mrs Armitage, Queen of the Road by Quentin Blake, Red Fox (0 099434 24 5)
Little Red Car by Nicola Baxter, 'Little Stories' series, Ladybird (0 721419 31 3) (and audio tape)

Non-fiction books:

Simple Machines – Wheels and Axles, Franklin Watts (0 749645 90 3)
Wheels by Henry Pluckrose, 'Readabouts' series, Franklin Watts (0 749652 76 4)

Music and songs:

'The Wheels on the Bus' (or any CD of popular children's songs)

Materials:

- Tyres
- Bicycle
- Cylindrical wooden blocks
- Selection of wheels and cogs
- Wood or stiff card to make ramps
- Sewing thread and large-eyed needles
- Threading laces
- Plain coloured fabrics
- Various different sized balls – for example, marbles, ping pong balls, tennis balls, rubber balls and inflatable balls
- Plastic hockey sticks
- Hoops

Wheels

Personal, Social and Emotional Development

 Be confident to initiate ideas and speak in a familiar group.

Circle time

- ❑ Introduce the word 'invention'. What does it mean? Tell the children that a long time ago the wheel was invented. Before that it must have been very difficult to move heavy objects. They had to be dragged or carried. Ask the children to think of as many objects and machines with wheels as they can.

- ❑ Consider other important inventions. Let the children take it in turns to describe something that is useful. For example, a washing machine – before it was invented, washing had to be done by hand and that was hard work; the aeroplane – we can travel to different countries all over the world.

Mathematical Development

 Begin to use vocabulary involved in adding and subtracting. Find one more or one less.

Patterns

- ❑ Make a collection of wheels and pictures of objects with wheels. Look closely at the patterns – spokes, cogs, hubcaps and size. Talk about the patterns – how spokes radiate from the centre and the shape of cog wheels. Look at tread patterns on tyres. Take rubbings of these patterns.

Counting

- ❑ Place ten wheels (such as Lego wheels) in a line. Count them. Then rearrange them. How many wheels are there? Rearrange them again. How many wheels do you see?

Adding and subtracting

- ❑ Add one more wheel. How many wheels are there now? Take one away. There is one less. How many wheels are there now? (Vary the numbers added or taken away according to the ability of the group.)

Extension

- ❑ Give each child ten counters. Ask them to take away a specified number. How many are left? Vary the number subtracted. Show the group how to represent this as a written sum (10 – 2 = 8).

Problem solving

- ❑ Show the children a toy car with detachable wheels. Say that most cars have four wheels. Remove one of the wheels and ask the children how many more wheels it needs. Remove different combinations of wheels and ask the children how many wheels are missing each time or how many more are needed.

Shape

- ❑ Remind the children about the shape of wheels. Tell them to look for other circles in the classroom (counters, lids and so on). Ask them to draw round the circles and cut them out. Use brightly coloured paper and make a collage of circles. They could be decorated using scraps of fabric and crayons. Use the collage for counting. For example, how many red circles can you see?

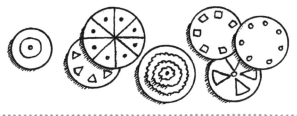

Outside

- ❑ Practise drawing circles in the sand tray, on the playground with large brushes and water, with wax crayons on paper and with paint, chalk or charcoal.

❑ Ask the children to stand in a circle. Try to make the circle really round. Choose a child to run around the circle, first clockwise and then anticlockwise.

Communication, Language and Literacy

 Retell narratives in the correct sequence.

Invite a visitor

❑ If possible, invite a car mechanic or someone who works in a garage to come and talk to the children about their work.

Listening

❑ Read a story about a car (see Resources). Ask the children questions about the story, such as: Which part did you like the best?

❑ Ask the children to help you to retell the story in sequence. Talk about what happened first, then what happened next and what happened at the end of the story.

❑ Ask the children to choose one part of the story and draw a picture of it on A3 paper. Add wide writing lines drawn about two-thirds of the sheet down. (The sheets could be photocopied to save time.)

Independent writing

❑ Help the children to put their pictures from the previous activity in order. Support them as they write sentences about their picture. Some could go over highlighter writing and others could copy underneath. The A3 pictures should be displayed so that visitors can read the story in sequence.

❑ Let them make labels for the stitched circles and printed wheel patterns (see Creative Development), such as 'cogs', 'spokes', 'hub', 'tyre', 'shaft' and 'axle'.

Rhyme

❑ Read the poem 'Gran's van' or 'My bike' (page 31). Ask the class to join in with you. Ask individual children to tell you the rhyming words.

❑ Can they think of other words to rhyme with 'cog' (log, dog, bog, frog), 'wheel' (steal, feel, meal, deal) and 'spoke' (woke, poke, folk, joke, soak)?

Knowledge and Understanding of the World

 Look closely at similarities, differences, patterns and change. Ask questions about why things happen and how things work.

Investigating spherical objects

❑ Provide a collection of objects such as wheels, rollers, hoops and marbles, with which the children can experiment freely.

❑ Provide a ramp, either in the role play garage or outside. As the children play, discuss rolling in a straight line. Ask: If you let a tennis ball and a marble go at the same time, which do you think will reach the bottom first? Which do you think will travel further? If you tip the ramp to make it a steeper hill, what do you think will happen?

Experimenting with rollers

❑ Challenge the children to move a large, heavy object, such as a container filled with sand, along the ground. Tie a cord around it and drag it. Is it easy to move? Ask them to think of ways to make the movement easier. Try putting it on a board with rollers or cylindrical wooden blocks underneath. Put it in a container with wheels. Which is easier? Why?

Wheels

What do they think would happen if the wheels were not round, but square or oval in shape?

Outside

Investigating a bicycle

❏ Push a bicycle along. Ask: What happens when the wheels turn? What happens when you pedal? Does a bicycle need petrol and an engine? Talk about pushing and pulling to make things move. If we push harder it moves faster. Turn the cycle upside down and spin the wheels. Ask: Can you still see the spokes? How can we safely stop the wheels turning? Talk about brakes.

Creative Development

Use their imagination in art and design.

Threading and sewing circular cards

❏ Make simple, laminated circular threading cards. Vary the sizes and distances between holes. Encourage the children to thread these with coloured laces and display them in the garage or classroom. More able children could attempt sewing running stitches around a circle drawn on fabric. (You will need sharp needles for this activity.)

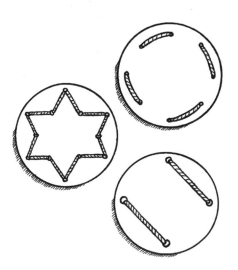

Printing with wheels

❏ Have some trays prepared with foam soaked in paint. Give each child a piece of plain fabric, a little larger than A4. Encourage them to make patterns by pressing wheels into the paint and printing on the fabric. Display with the sewing and threading.

Wheel collage

❏ You will need a piece of plain fabric, glue sticks and collage materials. Ask the children to make wheels to stick on the fabric. For example, pipe cleaner circles with spokes; drawn wheels, decorated and cut out; cog wheels; wheels drawn in pastel.

Drawing

❏ Invite the children to make observational drawings of a bicycle in pencil.

Music and song

❏ Sing 'The wheels on the bus go round and round'.

Physical Development

 Use a range of small and large equipment with increasing control.

Movement

❏ Explore twisting, turning, spinning and rolling movements. Tell the children to imagine they are steering wheels turning or car wheels spinning.

❏ Cutting skills: circles (see Mathematical Development).

Manipulation skills

❏ Practise rolling different sizes and shapes of balls to a partner. What happens when the ball is not round or has bits sticking out of it?

❏ Dribble balls around cones. Turn this into a game.

❏ If you have plastic hockey sticks, encourage the children to use them to take balls around the cones. If possible, develop this into a team game.

WEEK 3

The role play area

During this week the garage will be adapted to represent a car showroom. The children will take on the roles of car salespeople and customers and will practise using describing words and persuasive language to sell cars. They will make **advertising posters** and **junk model cars** and design **fantasy cars**. They will also program Roamer as a racing car.

advertising posters

fantasy car

junk model cars

Resources

Fiction books:

Duck in the Truck by Jez Alborough, Collins (0 006647 17 0)
Wheels by Shirley Hughes, Walker Books (0 744520 12 6)

Non-fiction books:

Follow the Map – My Car Journey, Franklin Watts (0 749644 43 5)
Busy Places – The Garage, Franklin Watts (0 749645 59 8)
Let's Go By Car, 'Little Nippers' series, Heinemann Library (0 431164 63 0)

Website:

Holding Hands, Kindescope www.kindescope.com

Music and songs:

Bobby Shaftoe, Clap Your Hands by Sue Nicholls, A&C Black (0 713635 56 8)
'Chitty, Chitty, Bang, Bang' on the cassette 'A Treasury of Children's Songs', Early Learning Centre (105157).

Materials:

- Jackets, waistcoats and ties
- Toy cars or other vehicles
- Metal objects such as nails, some ready coated with gloss paint
- Brochures from garage salesrooms
- Magazines and newspaper advertisements for cars
- Home-made cheque books
- Out-of-date plastic swipe cards
- Small plants
- Tables and chairs
- Roamer
- Road safety posters

A car showroom

Creative Development

Use their imagination in art and design.

Making the car showroom

❑ Support the children in changing the garage into a car showroom. Remove all inappropriate items and replace them with small tables and chairs for customers and salespeople to use. Invite the children to select different cars to display – both manufactured and home-made. Place flowers on the tables and provide cheque books for customers to use for payment (or plastic swipe cards).

Designing cars

❑ Discuss with the children their fantasy car. Ask: What would it do? How would it move? What features would you like to have – for example, wings, a back of seat television, a magic food machine or an umbrella to keep it dry?

❑ Ask the children to draw in pencil a design for their fantasy car. Encourage them to add as many details as possible, including a number plate. They should carefully add colour to their sketch. Encourage care and pride in their work. Mount the designs and display them on the background of the salesroom. Encourage groups of children to describe their cars and say what features they have added, and why.

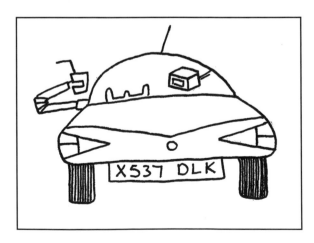

Observational drawings

❑ Either take the children into the school car park or give them a selection of toy vehicles. Ask them to look carefully and draw what they see. Do their drawings show the different shapes and features?

Model making

❑ Provide materials for the children to make junk models of cars.

❑ Dress Roamer as a fantasy car or racing car (see Mathematical Development). Help the children to select suitable collage materials.

Personal, Social and Emotional Development

Form good relations with adults and peers.

Circle time

❑ Tell the children how important it is for a car salesperson to make a good impression on potential clients. Talk about how we say 'Hello' and 'Good morning' to each other every day. Ask them how they feel when their friends say 'Hello' and smile at them.

❑ Explain to the class that a car salesperson will usually shake your hand when he or she meets you. It is a polite way of greeting and a way of introducing oneself. Practise this in the circle. Explain that we shake hands with our right hand. Ask the children to show you their right hand, then to take it in turns to stand up and cross the circle to shake hands with a friend. 'Hello Amir. I am George. How may I help you?'

Music and songs

❑ Sing the following exchange.

Teacher: Sophie, Sophie, where are you?
Sophie: Here I am. Here I am. How do you do?
Teacher and child shake hands.

❑ Sing 'The welcome song' and 'The goodbye song' at the end of the day, from *Bobby Shaftoe, Clap Your Hands* or 'Goodbye everybody' from *Holding Hands* (see Resources).

Mathematical Development

Use IT in problem solving. Count back reliably from 10. Begin to use the vocabulary of subtraction.

Programming Roamer to move forwards and backwards

❑ Mark out an area as a pit stop and another as a petrol pump.

❑ Make Roamer look like a racing car (see Creative Development) and ask the children to program it to move to the pit stop and the petrol pump, estimating distances as they go. Challenge them to bring Roamer back to the starting position.

Music and song

❑ Sing 'Ten speedy racing cars' (page 31).

Extension

❑ Work out the differences between prices of cars. For example, if I bring my old car in to sell at £10 in part exchange for a car which costs £20, how much more will I have to pay? (Prices should be kept within the capability of the children.)

Communication, Language and Literacy

Listen with enjoyment and respond to stories.

Listening

❑ Ask a car sales representative to talk about their work.

❑ Read a story about cars (see Resources). Talk about the story, encouraging the children to recall events.

❑ Show them a non-fiction book about cars and point out the differences between fiction and non-fiction. Do the children prefer a story or information book?

Viewing

❑ If possible, show excerpts from *Chitty Chitty Bang Bang*. Discuss the special features the car had. Could there really be a flying car?

Talking for a particular purpose

❑ Take groups of children into the role play showroom. Decide who is going to be the salesperson and who are going to be customers. The salesperson could wear a smart suit and a tie. Demonstrate how to describe one of the fantasy cars, using persuasive language to encourage someone to 'buy'. For example, 'This car' – quote the registration number – 'has very comfortable seats. It goes very fast and even has a refrigerator in the boot to keep your sandwiches fresh and cool for a picnic at the end of a long journey!'

Phonics

❑ Ask the children to tell you the initial sound of the following words – 'car', 'bus', 'room', 'man' and 'wheel'. Invite individual children to come and write the initial letter on the board.

❑ Ask the children to tell you the final sound in the following words – 'man', 'stop', 'bus', 'cat', 'dog', 'cab', 'lad', 'cliff', 'hill', 'him' and 'put'. Ask the children to write the final letter on their whiteboards.

Extension

❑ Ask the group to sound out the three phonemes in the following words – 'mat', 'pet', 'hit', 'hot' and 'cut'.

Writing: teacher scribing – creating posters

❑ Look at advertisements from magazines, newspapers and brochures. Tell the class they are going to make a poster for the showroom. Ask them what words they might need ('sale', 'bargain', 'excellent condition' and so on). Write these on the board and talk about the letter formation.

❑ Ask the children to suggest slogans for their cars; for example, 'More power', 'More room' and 'More luxury'. Write these on the board and talk about the writing process as you write.

Independent writing

❑ Tell the children to cut out a picture of a car from a magazine or brochure. Support them as they add 'selling' words around it, using the words you wrote on the board as a model, such as 'heated rear window' and 'alarm'. Display these in the showroom or around the classroom.

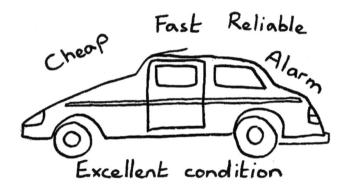

Extension

❑ Invite the children to write slogans on strips of card to persuade people to buy their cars. Display these in the showroom.

Knowledge and Understanding of the World

 Look closely at similarities, differences and change.

Music and song

❑ Sing the song 'Twinkle twinkle chocolate bar' (page 31).

Investigating rust

❑ Talk about rust. What things can go rusty? Why is rust a nuisance on a car? Ask the children if they have seen a rusty car.

❑ Experiment with metal objects, such as nails, in water. Ask: What happened to the nail? How long did it take before it started to rust? How could we protect metal from rusting? Explain that cars are painted not just to look good but also to protect them from rusting.

❑ Do further experiments with a painted nail, an oily nail, a nail in salty water, a nail enclosed in cling film or a polythene bag and an unpainted nail. Leave one nail out of the water. Which nail went rusty first?

Road safety

❑ Talk about road safety. Remind the children about safe places to cross the road. Talk about looking and listening when they cross. Look at posters for the Green Cross Code and in the playground practise crossing when there are no vehicles coming.

Physical Development

 Move with control and coordination.

Movement

❑ Give the children instructions to move in different ways. For example, to move like an old car: jerkily, stopping and starting. Move like a racing car: fast, turning corners quickly. Move like a lorry: heavily, in pairs. Move like a coach: heavily, in pairs in a line.

Playing racing cars

❑ Stand the children in a circle, facing inwards. In threes, name each child – for example, Ferrari, Jaguar and Mini. Call out one name. Those children step back onto the 'track'. Show them the direction they will be travelling. 1st gear – walk slowly, 2nd gear – faster, 3rd gear – faster still, 4th gear – running, and then back down through the gears. Reverse – move backwards. Pit stop – stand still. Race for the finish – run as fast as you can back to your place in the circle. (They MUST NOT change direction when running back to their place in the circle.)

WEEK 4

The role play area

During this week the role play area will be adapted to represent the inside of an airport. The children will create the **background** of the airport, including the **runway** and **runway lights**, paint **pictures of planes** and **posters of holiday destinations**. They will make passports, using a digital camera, and plane tickets. The check-in area will have a **desk**, **luggage weighing area** and **moving belt**. In role play, the children will re-enact going to the airport, checking in luggage and using their passports. Support their imaginative play by participating in their role play.

Resources

Photocopiables:

Poems and songs 2 (page 32)
Flight tickets and boarding passes (page 33)

Fiction books:

Eugene and the Plane Spotter by Katherine Lodge, Bloomsbury (0 747549 86 9)
Amazing Aeroplanes by Tony Mitton, Kingfisher (0 753407 22 1)

Non-fiction books:

Aeroplane by Caroline Bingham, 'Machines at Work' series, Dorling Kindersley (0 751364 96 7)
Planes by F Patchett, 'Usborne Beginners' series, Usborne (0 746045 45 X)

Music and songs:

'Helpers' from *The Handy Band* by Sue Nicholls, A&C Black (0 713668 97 0)

Materials:

- Pictures and posters of aeroplanes and airports
- Photographs taken in an airport of check-in, departures etc.
- A set of bathroom scales
- A few small suitcases
- Items of clothing, beach towels and shoes, to fold and pack
- An old passport
- World or Europe outline map (GLS supply playcloth maps)
- A globe
- Travel brochures and posters from travel agents
- Aprons and overalls
- Dressing-up clothes for passengers
- Tabards for uniforms
- Till rolls
- Small construction bricks
- Playmobil people, or similar
- Telephone and digital camera
- Identical cut-out aeroplane shapes or Mini Motors aeroplanes (GLS Educational Supplies, www.glsed.co.uk)
- School stamp and other small stamps
- Ink pad

Creating an airport

Knowledge and Understanding of the World

Find out and ask questions about why things happen and how things work.

Introducing airports

❑ If possible, provide pictures of the inside of an airport. Introduce and explain new vocabulary and terminology, such as 'check-in', 'baggage belts', 'passport control', 'security', 'announcements' and 'delays'. Ask the children if they have ever been to an airport. Ask: What buildings are there? Who works there? What jobs do they do? Who wears a uniform? How does the luggage get to the plane? How do you know your flight is ready for take-off?

❑ Consider the speed of air travel compared with journeys by car or by sea. Look at a globe. Ask where the children have travelled to or where they would like to travel to. Why is it better to travel to some places by plane?

Passports

❑ Look at a real passport. Talk about why we need to take our passport when we visit other countries. Passports show which country we come from. They are proof of who we are. Tell the children that they are going to make their own passports to use in the role play area. Ask them to think what they will need to put in them – for example, their name and date of birth, a photograph and a number.

Creative Development

 Explore colour, texture, shape, form and space in two and three dimensions.

Creating the background of the airport

Sky

❑ Sponge print with shades of blue paint onto either blue or white paper. Use this to line one wall. Alternatively, if using drapes to create the role play area, choose a light blue or white fabric. (Sheeting works well.)

❑ Paint pictures of aeroplanes, cut them out and mount them on the sky background.

Check-in desk

❑ Convert a table or box from the 'garage' into a check-in desk. If possible, have another, box below it to it to represent the luggage belt. Place scales for weighing the luggage beside the desk.

Departure lounge

❑ Provide chairs for the children in the departure lounge. When their flight is called they should bring their passports to be stamped and receive their boarding passes (see Communication, Language and Literacy).

❑ Provide a telephone, writing tools and paper in the airport for the ground staff to use.

Runway

❑ Use A1 sheets of paper or lining paper to create the background. Paint wet on wet blues merging into a sand colour, top to bottom. When dry, paint a runway running horizontally across the sand background. Add a strip of green for grass at the bottom of the painting. Add a line of runway lights made out of lolly sticks and brightly coloured paper. Draw airport buildings, such as a hangar and control tower. Cut them out and stick them on the background.

Making an aeroplane

❑ Ask a child to draw a large aeroplane on some stiff card. Cut it out and tape screwed-up newspaper

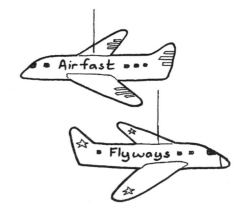

over the body of the plane. Cover the whole plane with kitchen paper using PVA glue. As you add layers of kitchen paper, smooth the surface. When dry, paint and mount at an angle (as if taking off) along the runway.

❑ Other walls or display areas could be decorated with pictures and posters from travel agents. Have some brochures in the airport for the children to browse through.

Designing a livery for an airline

❑ Show pictures of aircraft from different airlines. Give the children a template of an aeroplane to draw round on card. Ask them to cut it out and design markings to match on both sides. Encourage them to think of a name for their airline and write it on the plane. Suspend these from the ceiling in the role play area.

Construction play

❑ With small bricks or Lego, construct a terminal building. Do not put a roof on the building so that the children can see inside. Ask: Where will the passengers get into the terminal? Do the little people fit through the door? Can you build different areas inside your building?

Personal, Social and Emotional Development

 Understand that people need to be treated with respect.

Circle time

❑ Invite discussion about people who work in an airport. Talk about how everybody's jobs are important. For example, cleaners are important because if they didn't sweep the floors or clean the tables the airport would look dirty. Ask the children if they would like to work in an airport and what job they would like to do.

❑ Ask the children to help you to make a list of all the people who work in school. Talk about the important jobs everyone does.

❑ Sing the song 'Helpers' (see Resources). Adjust the words to suit your school's situation.

Mathematical Development

 Use language such as 'heavier' or 'lighter' to compare quantities.

Comparison of weight

❑ Place a set of bathroom scales by the luggage belt at the check-in. You will need suitcases containing objects of different weights. Encourage the children to weigh the suitcases. Talk about kilograms. Does your case weigh more or less than a kilogram? Whose case is heaviest? Try estimating first and then use the scales to find out.

Estimating

❑ Pack a suitcase. Provide clothing and bulky objects, such as beach towels and shoes. Discuss whether the pile of clothes will fit in the suitcase. Try it. Talk about folding the clothes (show them how to fold the clothes neatly) and packing them carefully.

❑ Experiment with packing a large suitcase with a few light items and a small case with heavy items. Ask which case will be heavier. Check on the scales.

❑ Have ready some identically sized small aeroplane shapes cut out of coloured card and laminated, or Mini Motors planes (available from GLS – see Resources). Also have ready some different length strips of card to represent runways. Ask the children to guess how many aeroplanes will fit nose to tail along each runway. Check to see if they are right.

Measuring

❑ Provide strips of paper or till rolls. Challenge the children to measure and cut a runway exactly the length of a ruler, a book or a table.

Extension

❑ Ask the group to record the measurements. They should write, 'The ... was ... cm. The longest object was ... cm. The shortest object was ... cm.'

Outside

❑ Draw runway strips in chalk on the playground. Use strides to measure the length of each runway.

Creating an airport

Communication, Language and Literacy

 Use talk to organise, sequence and clarify thinking, ideas and events.

Listening

❑ Show the children a non-fiction book about an airport (see Resources). Ask them to think of something they would like to know about an airport and show them how to use the contents page and the index to find the information. Leave the book in the role play area for the children to refer to.

Writing: teacher scribing

❑ Scribe labels for the children to copy, such as 'Check-in Desk', 'Departures', 'Arrivals', 'Passport Control', 'Toilets' and a sign above check-in for the airline (this could be the class or school name).

Talking

❑ Discuss possible questions a passenger might be asked at check-in. For example, Can I see your ticket and passport please? Where are you travelling to? Did you pack your case yourself? Has your luggage been left unattended? (Explain the terminology.)

Rhyme

❑ Sing the song 'Down at the airport' (page 32) to the class. Let them join in as you sing it again.

Independent writing

❑ Have prepared some passport-sized books made with card covers (possibly coloured) and just two paper pages. Help the children to take digital photos of each other. Print these out thumbnail size. Tell them to stick the photo in the book and help them to write their full name and other information on the back page. On the front cover, write 'My Passport'. Store them in a box in the role play area. When they enter the passport control area they should take their passports to be stamped.

Extension

❑ More able children can use the computer to print their details. Stick these inside their passports.

Tickets

❑ Photocopy page 33 onto thin card and cut it out. Give each child a ticket. Show them how to write on their tickets and use them in their role play.

Boarding passes

❑ Give each child a boarding pass (page 33) and ask them to write on it the gate, the row and the seat number – for example, Gate 20, Row 6, Seat A.

Map reading

❑ Provide a large map of either the world or Europe. Select six destinations – for example, London, New York, Paris, Hong Kong, Sydney and Delhi. Write these names on pieces of card. Help the children to find these places on a globe. Challenge them to find the correct places to put them on the map. Fix the cards on the map with sticky tack.

Physical Development

 Recognise the changes that happen to their bodies when they are active.

Movement

❑ Pretend to carry a heavy suitcase, run to catch a plane, walk busily, clean the floor and so on.
❑ Pretend to be baggage handlers putting suitcases onto the trailer. Encourage the children to describe how they feel. Do they feel puffed out? Are their hearts beating fast?

WEEK 5

The role play area

During this week the children will learn about the outside of the airport. They will create a **mini role play area** in the form of an airport layout and use this to explore the workings of an airport. They will make **paper aeroplanes**, record airport announcements and send Roamer around the airport buildings.

– paper aeroplanes

mini role play area

Resources

Photocopiables:

Poems and songs 2 (page 32)
A pop-up airport (page 34)
Paper aeroplanes (page 35)

Fiction book:

Bruno and the New Plane by C and J Hawkins, Orchard Books (1 843622 59 9)

Non-fiction books:

Air and Flight by Sally Hewitt, 'It's Science' series, Franklin Watts (0 749645 11 3)
Let's Go By Plane, 'Little Nippers' series, Heinemann Library (0 431164 64 9)

Music and songs:

Holding Hands, Kindescope (book and CD), www.kindescope.com

Materials:

- Map jigsaws
- Different coloured card cut into 10cm circles
- Large sheet of stiff card or hardboard
- Playmobil people
- Torch
- Mini Motors aeroplanes (GLS)
- Lego
- Tape recorder
- Roamer
- Collage materials such as lolly sticks, matchsticks, card tubes, sponge, beads and lids
- Boxes of various sizes
- PE bats or table tennis bats
- Egg timers

Making models

Knowledge and Understanding of the World

 Find out and identify the uses of technology.

Class discussion

❑ Talk about what happens outside the terminal building. If possible, look at pictures, posters and non-fiction books. Discuss runways and taxiways, and the noise on landing and take-off. Talk about air traffic control and radar. Explain how planes need aviation fuel and that this is piped into the tanks from fuel tankers.

ICT

❑ Show the children how to operate the tape recorder, using the stop, play and volume control buttons. Explain that they will be making airport announcements.

Creative Development

 Express and communicate their ideas, using a widening range of materials and techniques.

Making pop-ups

❑ Make a pop-up airport scene (see page 34).

Paper aeroplanes

❑ Provide a selection of paper of different thicknesses and sizes. Show the children how to fold the paper to make a simple aeroplane and test it (see page 35). Ask them to have a go at making their own planes and testing them. Ask: Whose plane flies the furthest? Whose plane flies in a straight line? Challenge the children to adapt their planes to fly further. (Younger children may just follow your instructions to make a plane.) Suspend them from the ceiling in the role play area.

Mini role play area

❑ You will need as large a sheet of stiff card as possible (for example, discarded display boards from your local video shop or a sheet of hardboard), a selection of boxes (sorted by size and available on different tables) and a selection of collage materials such as lolly sticks, matchsticks, small card tubes, sponge, beads and lids. Ask the children to design the layout of the airport, inviting ideas from all the class. Ask a group to draw the design on the board. (NB: you may need to cover the board with paper first.)

❑ Talk about scale. Which will be the biggest building? Will the cars be as big as the buildings?

Group activities

❑ Ask different groups of children to take responsibility for the following aspects of construction.

 – Paint the main features, such as the runways, green areas, areas for buildings, car park and roads leading to the airport.

 – Make the airport terminal, air traffic control and other small buildings out of boxes.

 – Make planes out of small tubes and card.

 – Make vehicles such as luggage trailers, fire engines, cars and coaches.

 – Make trees and shrubs out of pieces of foam, lolly sticks, matchsticks, paper and so on.

 – Make luggage out of air-hardening clay, tiny boxes, Lego and so on.

❑ Glue the buildings and other fixtures to the board. Place the vehicles appropriately and encourage free imaginative play.

Communication, Language and Literacy

 Use language to imagine and recreate roles and experiences.

Writing: teacher scribing

❑ Add labels or annotate the pop-up airport scenes (see Creative Development). Scribe for the children or let them copy the labels. Encourage the more able to have a go at their own writing. Write labels such as 'runway', 'taking off', 'coming in to land' and 'passengers'.

Speaking and listening: recording announcements

❑ Following discussion about announcements they might hear at an airport, encourage individuals to record a short announcement on a tape recorder. For example, 'The flight to Paris has been delayed until 10 o'clock,', 'Please keep your luggage with you at all times,' and 'The flight to London is now boarding.' Leave a gap of approximately 30 seconds between each announcement. Leave the completed tape running in the role play area. Encourage the children to listen and respond to the announcements in their imaginative play. You may need to model this. (It is advisable to remove the tabs on the tape to prevent inadvertent overrecording!)

Phonics

❑ Draw a phoneme frame on the board (*Progression in Phonics* PCM 1 or 2). Demonstrate how to fit the phonemes of a word into the frame. Start with three-letter words, such as 'bag', and progress to words that start with a digraph, such as 'ch' or 'sh'; for example, 'chin' and 'shop'. Draw the children's attention to the fact that two letters go in the one phoneme box.

c h	i	n
s h	o	p

Listening

❑ Read a story to the class (see Resources) and then discuss it. Ask groups of children to freeze-frame incidents in the story. Ask the others to suggest what the characters are doing.

❑ Perform together a poem or song from page 32.

Mathematical Development

 Recognise and recreate simple patterns.

Map jigsaws

❑ Encourage the children to do jigsaws of maps (available from most educational catalogues or see websites). Talk about the different countries.

Sequencing runway lights

❑ You will need circles of different coloured card fixed to the wall of the role play area or classroom, and a torch. Explain that you will give a sequence of colours such as red, blue, green and that the torch should be shone on those colours, in that order. Change the sequence. For example, blue, blue, yellow, blue. Make the sequence challenging according to ability. Challenge the children to continue the sequence. Which colour comes next?

❑ Make a second set of colour sequence circles. Ask a child to shuffle the circles and then call out the sequence for a partner to follow with the torch.

Counting

❑ You will need Mini Motors aeroplanes and the card planes from last week (or the planes made by the children for the model airport layout – see Creative Development). On the layout, place ten aircraft around the terminal building. Then take one of the planes and put it on the runway. How many planes are still at the terminal? How many planes altogether? Vary this activity, exploring number conservation and number bonds. For example, put two planes on the runway, six at the terminal and two in the air.

Making models

Extension

❏ Discuss with the children ways of recording the above. Show them how to divide their whiteboards into three columns and label the columns 'runway' 'terminal' and 'air'. Ask them to record the numbers as other children change the planes' positions.

Music and song

❏ Sing 'Down at the airport' (see page 32).

ICT – Roamer

❏ Place two pieces of card on the floor, one labelled 'car park', the other labelled 'terminal building'. Fix a small box to the top of Roamer. Ask the children to take passengers (perhaps play people) from the car park to the terminal building. Alternatively, label small pieces of Lego to transport as luggage from the terminal to an aircraft.

Personal, Social and Emotional Development

 Consider the consequences of their actions for themselves and others.

Class discussion: tidying up

❏ Talk to the class about people whose job it is to keep the airport tidy. Explain that they work both day and night. If possible, show them pictures of sweepers and floor polishers. Explain the importance of keeping the classroom tidy. Explain how this helps stop things being broken and makes it easy to find things if they have been put away in the right place and ready for the next person to use. Discuss the following: Who should tidy up? What would happen if we didn't all help to tidy up? What would happen to our equipment and toys? Make this a positive discussion.

Music and song

❏ Sing 'Pick up the toys' from *Holding Hands* (see Resources).

Physical Development

 Show awareness of space. Move with control.

Aircraft landing

❏ Talk about how pilots follow signals directing them to the terminal building after landing. Provide small bats or cut-out card paddles. Demonstrate how to give instructions using the bats such as 'go left' (point to the left) and 'come forward' (beckon with both bats). Divide the class into groups. Give one child in each group a pair of bats. Challenge them to make signals for the group to follow.

Outside
Following oral instructions

❏ If possible, have a toy mobile phone or radio-telephone. On the playground, draw out in chalk a simple track or course. Give one child the radio-telephone and blindfold another. The child with the radio-telephone gives instructions to the other to help him or her negotiate the course. For example, 'Take two steps forward, turn right, three steps forward' and so on. (It might be advisable for you to walk alongside younger children.)

WEEK 6

The role play area

During this week the role play area will become the inside of an aeroplane. The children will learn about the people who work on board an aeroplane. They will consider the needs of the passengers and find out about some cultural changes on landing in another country. They will make a **cockpit** and in-flight food for their passengers. They will also design a **uniform** for a steward or stewardess and make a **pilot's hat** to wear as they role play the flight.

Resources

Photocopiables:

Paper aeroplanes (page 35)
Fairy cakes and in-flight food (page 36)
Steward and stewardess (page 37)
Costumes (page 38)

Fiction book:

Topsy and Tim Go on an Aeroplane by Jean and Gareth Adamson, Ladybird (1 904351 28 X)

Non-fiction book:

A Day in the Life of a Flight Attendant, Franklin Watts (0 749641 09 6)

Music and songs:

Bingo Lingo by Helen MacGregor, A&C Black (0 713650 75 3)
Tom Thumb's Musical Maths by Helen MacGregor, A&C Black (0 713649 71 2)
'Summer holiday' by Cliff Richard
'Leaving on a jet plane' by John Denver

Materials:

- Tabards, hats and aprons
- Shallow boxes such as cereal boxes or trays
- Small food containers/boxes/foil dishes
- Clip belt (possibly from a child's car seat)
- Play dough or air-hardening modelling clay
- Serviettes
- Plastic knives, forks, spoons
- Plastic cups
- Eye masks
- Small blankets
- Neck support pillows
- An old tea trolley, if you can get hold of one
- Postcards
- School address labels
- Large box (if possible, the size of a washing machine)
- Tinfoil
- Lids
- Plain card cut larger than a normal postcard
- Currency of different countries

Inside the plane

Personal, Social and Emotional Development

 Respond to significant experiences, showing a range of feelings.

Circle time: exploring feelings

❑ Ask the children if they have ever been to an airport to meet someone. Ask: Who did you meet? How did you feel when you saw them come through 'arrivals'? Have you ever been to an airport to say cheerio to someone you love? How did you feel then? If you felt sad, what comforted you or made you feel better? Talk about how it feels to be at an airport, waiting to go on holiday. Talk about excitement and feeling impatient.

Music and songs

❑ Sing 'Goodbye everybody' and 'Cuddle teddy' from *Holding Hands* (see Resources).

Mathematical Development

 Recognising patterns in number.

Estimating

❑ Talk about the small space for a lot of people on aircraft. Provide a selection of small containers and sorting objects, such as Mini Motors. Ask the children to estimate how many items will fit in each container, then to try it and see. Were they right?

Counting in twos

❑ Set out two rows of chairs and sit children on them. Tell the others that they are going to count. Do this by counting in ones and then show them counting in twos. Use a number square to illustrate. Practise counting in twos, using Unifix.

Extension

❑ Challenge the children to count in threes. They could mark every third number on a number square.

Measuring accurately

❑ See fairy cake making (Creative Development).

Communication, Language and Literacy

 Know that print carries meaning.

Signs and signals on board

❑ Demonstrate some of the instructions, signs and signals given by cabin crews – for example, pointing out the emergency exits. Ask the children to copy your signals.

Rhyme

❑ Sing 'Captain of the aeroplane' from *Bingo Lingo* (see Resources). Identify the rhyming words and make up actions.

Writing postcards: teacher modelling

❑ You will need old postcards, ready-cut cards and school address labels (photocopied or printed on the computer). Look at a few postcards from various places. Ask: Why do people send postcards? Can you think of a place you have visited? Did you have a good time there? Invite discussion about different holidays and destinations.

❑ Draw a large card on the class board. Decide on a location. It may be the seaside or a city. Ask the children to help you draw a picture of this place on the card. Explain that this is the front of the card and that we write on the back. Draw another blank card. Discuss where the address and the message should be written. Demonstrate writing a typical postcard message – 'Wish you were here.' What else do we need (a stamp)? Tell the children that they are going to make postcards to send to the school.

Writing: teacher scribing

❑ Ask the children to suggest a simple sentence to write on their postcard, such as, 'I am having a lovely time at the seaside. Love Matthew'. Give each child a larger than normal postcard and ask them to draw a picture on the front. Draw a vertical line down the back. They can write their message and then stick on an address label. Finally, ask them to design a stamp in the top right-hand corner. Display these in the airport. You could suspend some of them from the ceiling.

Knowledge and Understanding of the World

 Begin to know about their own cultures and those of other people.

Discussion

❑ Discuss with the children the services on board a plane. Ask: Who flies and controls the plane? Whose job is it to make sure it goes in the right direction? Who looks after the passengers? What do they do?

❑ Talk about safety on board – wearing seat belts and emergency exits.

❑ Talk about different languages in the context of landing in another country. Do any of the children know how to say hello in French or Spanish?

❑ Talk about different currencies. If possible, show the children some and compare the notes and coins to ours.

Music and songs

❑ Sing 'Hello around the world' from *Bingo Lingo* and 'Three around the world' from *Tom Thumb's Musical Maths* (see Resources).

Creative Development

 Use their imagination in art and design.

In-flight catering

(Carry out this activity the day before the tray filling activity below.)

❑ Explain to the children that they are in-flight caterers. They are going to make some fairy cakes to put in meal trays. Explain that the cakes need to

be quite small to fit in the trays with the other food. In manageable groups, make the cakes. Everyone should at least get a turn to stir the mixture! (See page 36.)

Creating an in-flight meal tray

❑ Provide a bowl of chopped fruits, bread, butter or spread, sandwich fillings (jam, Marmite and so on), knives, spoons and fairy cakes. In groups, give each child a shallow box, such as a cereal box, with the front cut out. Ask them to write their name on the side. Tell them that this is their meal tray and that they should make their own meal for a journey on board an aircraft. They need to make a chopped fruit starter, a sandwich and a pudding – all to fit into small containers in the tray. They should also include a serviette, a cup and some cutlery.

Designing a uniform for a flight attendant

❑ Give each child a copy of pages 37 and 38 (figures and clothing worn by flight attendants). Ask them to colour, decorate and cut out the items of clothing they wish to use and then glue them onto the figures. They should add their own designs for hats, shoes and badges.

Making the cockpit of a plane

❑ See page 35 for instructions on how to make a cockpit. Encourage the children to take on the roles of pilot and aircrew. They can sit on the floor in front of the controls.

Making a pilot's hat

❑ See page 35 for a instructions.

Inside the plane

Time for take-off!

(This makes a good end-of-unit activity.)

❑ Make rows of chairs to represent the inside of an aircraft. Have a chair for each child. You or another adult should take on the role of the flight attendant. Show the children to their seats. Give some children neck support pillows, blankets and eye masks. In the role of flight attendant, announce 'Welcome aboard this jumbo jet. We shall arrive in Paris at two o'clock. First, there are some important announcements.' Go through a very short safety routine! Fasten your seat belts and off you go!

❑ Play Cliff Richard's 'Summer Holiday' and/or 'Leaving on a jet plane' by John Denver as in-flight entertainment (see Resources).

❑ Meanwhile announce the meal. If possible, use a tea trolley to carry the meal trays between the chairs; otherwise slide them along on a large box! As the children eat their meals, pour fruit juice into their cups. Stay in role but take the opportunity to talk about how difficult it is to eat a meal in such a small space, what you can see out of the window and so on!

Physical Development

 Handle objects with increasing control. Move with control and coordination.

Pouring with control

❑ Talk about pouring liquid from a large jug into a small cup on an aircraft while it is moving. Do the children think it is easy to do without spilling any on the passengers? Provide some small cups or beakers and some large plastic jugs in the water tray. Allow time for the children to practise pouring. Then

suggest they try doing the same activity while moving from side to side.

Flying and banking: mirroring movements

❑ Play a game of 'Simon says'. Stand in front of the children, who should be sitting in rows as on an aircraft. As the plane turns or banks, lean to one side and ask the children to mirror this. Sometimes be still; sometimes bounce and move as if there is turbulence.

❑ Divide the children into groups. Ask them to take it in turns to be the leader and tell the group to mirror the leader's movements. Ask the groups to show each other what they have been doing.

Outside

Moving accurately

❑ Draw narrow pathways in chalk on the playground. Explain that the pathways are rather like the narrow aisles on board a plane. Challenge the children to walk along the pathways without going over the edge. Make some of the paths very narrow so that the children have to keep their concentration and balance.

Review and evaluation

Encourage the children to reflect on the topic. What have they enjoyed learning about? Which part has been most exciting? Which stories and songs do they remember? Which artwork did they most enjoy doing? Would they like to work in a garage or travel on a plane?

Gran's van

My old Gran
Has a tumbledown van.
It rattles along
Like an old tin can.
A man called Dan
Tried to mend Gran's van,
With a broken spanner
And a frying pan!

Cynthia Rider

Twinkle twinkle chocolate bar

Twinkle twinkle chocolate bar
My son drives a rusty car,
Push the lever
Pull the choke
Off we go in a cloud of smoke.
Twinkle twinkle chocolate bar
My son drives a rusty car.

Anon

Ten speedy racing cars

(to the tune of 'John Brown's body')

Ten speedy racing cars went zooming round
the track *(x3)*
Then one had a flat tyre and had to go back.

What a shame it had to happen *(x3)*
One had a flat tyre and had to go back.

*(Continue with nine, eight, seven and so on. The
children may think of other reasons for the cars to
go back.)*

One speedy racing car went zooming round
the track *(x3)*
He passed the winning post. Fancy that!

Maggie Hutchings

Garage mechanic's song

(to the tune of 'She'll be coming round the mountain')

If you bring your car to us we'll fix it quick
(quick, quick)

If you bring your car to us we'll fix it quick
(quick, quick)

If you bring your car to us, bring your car to
us

Bring your car to us we'll fix it quick (double,
quick)

If your car tyre's flat we'll pump it up (pump,
pump)

If your car tyre's flat we'll pump it up (pump,
pump)

…and so on

Dee Reid

My bike

I never make a fuss
On a bus.
I never am a pain
On a train
Or a plane.
I never set the goat
Afloat
In a boat.
I never go too far
In a car.
I like
My bike.

John Kitching

Poems and songs 2

Down at the airport

(to the tune of 'Down at the station')

Down at the airport
Early in the morning
See all the aeroplanes standing in a row.
See them on the runway.
(Show number with fingers.)
See them at the terminal.
(As above.)
Brrm, brrm, brrm, brrm
And off they go!

Down at the airport
Early in the morning
See all the passengers standing in a row.
See them at the check in.
See them in the car park.
Brrm, brrm, brrm, brrm
And off they go!

(Children could make up their own verses.)

Maggie Hutchings

Looping the loop

Zooperty zoometry zoop,
the aeroplane's looping the loop.
It's zooming up,
it's zooming down,
it's zooming high
above the town.

Charles Thomson

Aeroplanes, aeroplanes

Aeroplanes, aeroplanes, look where they fly.
Aeroplanes, aeroplanes, high in the sky.
Their engines are noisy, they make a loud hum.
Now I'm a plane. Look out! Here I come!

Barbara Ireson

Taking off

The aeroplane taxies down the field
And heads into the breeze,
It lifts its wheels above the ground,
It skims above the trees,
It rises higher and higher
Away towards the sun,
It's just a speck against the sky
– and now it's gone.

Anon

The aeroplane goes up, up, up

(to the tune of 'London Bridge is falling down')

The aeroplane goes up, up, up
Up, up, up, up, up, up
The aeroplane goes up, up, up
Into the sky.

The aeroplane can loop the loop
Loop the loop, loop the loop
The aeroplane can loop the loop
In the sky.

Now the plane is coming down
Coming down, coming down
Now the plane is coming down
Landing safely.

Dee Reid

Tickets and boarding passes

OUT Flight ticket

Name ______________________________

From ______________ to ______________

Flight time ____________

____________ **Airlines**

IN Flight ticket

Name ______________________________

From ______________ to ______________

Flight time ____________

____________ **Airlines**

Boarding pass

Gate number ☐ Row ☐ Seat letter ☐

____________ **Airlines**

Boarding pass

Gate number ☐ Row ☐ Seat letter ☐

____________ **Airlines**

A pop-up airport

Instructions for making a pop-up airport

You will need:

- A3 paper
- A3 card

Fold the paper in half. Draw six lines for the children to cut to create the three pop-ups. (Figure 1)

Open up the paper, pull out the pop-ups and refold them outwards. (As in Figure 3)

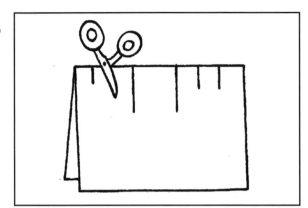

Figure 1

On separate pieces of paper, the children can draw passengers, planes, the buildings, luggage and so on. Cut them out and glue to the pop-ups to give a 3-D effect. (Figure 2)

Flatten the paper so that the children can add details on the background, such as the runway, clouds and a plane coming in to land.

Figure 2

Fold the paper. Recreate the pop-ups and place the picture inside a folded sheet of A3 card to strengthen the scene. (Figure 3)

Figure 3

How to make a paper aeroplane

You will need:
• a piece of A5 paper

What to do:
1. Fold in two corners to make a point.
2. Fold paper in half lengthways.
3. Fold each wing from nose to tail.
4. Fold each wing again from nose to tail to align with bottom of the wing.

How to make a cockpit

You will need:
• a very large box (possibly from a washing machine)
• lids
• collage materials

• smaller boxes
• white paint
• black sugar paper

1. Cut a window out of a very large box. Paint the box white inside and out. Leave the back open.
2. Cover one or two smaller boxes with black sugar paper and add knobs, dials and levers for the controls (using lids and collage materials).
3. Ask the children to think of their own ideas for the controls. Glue or staple the control panels in the box.
4. Add clipboards and pencils.

How to make a pilot's hat

You will need:
• strips of dark blue or black firm paper or thin card, stapled into a band to fit a child's head
• circles of paper, cut a slightly larger diameter than the stapled strips (snip into the circles all the way around)
• semicircles of card for peaks
• sticky tape
• gold, silver and other shiny paper

1. Assemble the hats with the children. Show them how to fold under the edge of the circles and help them to stick them to the inside of the headbands. Snip the straight edge of the semicircles and fix to the bands to make a peak.
2. Ask the children to decorate the hats with shiny paper. They could make a badge or wings for the front or a coloured strip around the band.

Fairy cakes

Ingredients
250g margarine
250g castor sugar
250g self raising flour
2 large eggs, whisked
1 tsp baking powder
A few drops of vanilla essence
Icing sugar
Hundreds-and-thousands (or similar)

Method
1. Cream the margarine and sugar together.
2. Mix in the eggs and vanilla essence. Add a little of the flour to prevent curdling.
3. Sift in the rest of the flour and the baking powder.
4. Mix well.
5. Spoon the mixture into *petit four* cake cases and bake for 5 to 6 minutes in a moderate oven.
6. Make icing, using icing sugar and water, and decorate the cakes when cold. Store in a tin.

In flight food
- Put chopped fruit in small containers or use dried fruit.
- Cut slices of buttered bread into small squares. Add fillings, such as jam or cheese spread.
- Collect salt, pepper and sugar sachets.
- Fairy cakes (see above).

Photocopiable

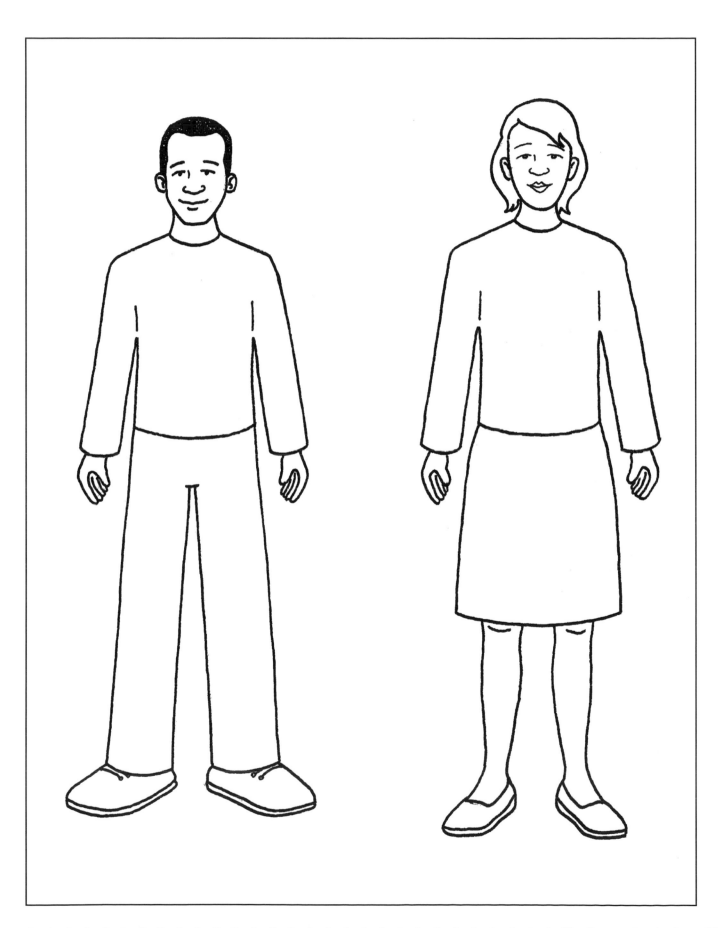

Observational Assessment Chart

Unit: _____   Class: _____   Date: _____

Name	Personal, Social and Emotional Development	Communication, Language and Literacy	Knowledge & Understanding of the World	Mathematical Development	Creative Development	Physical Development
	Y B G ELG	Y B G ELG	Y B G ELG	Y B G ELG	Y B G ELG	Y B G ELG
	Y B G ELG	Y B G ELG	Y B G ELG	Y B G ELG	Y B G ELG	Y B G ELG
	Y B G ELG	Y B G ELG	Y B G ELG	Y B G ELG	Y B G ELG	Y B G ELG
	Y B G ELG	Y B G ELG	Y B G ELG	Y B G ELG	Y B G ELG	Y B G ELG
	Y B G ELG	Y B G ELG	Y B G ELG	Y B G ELG	Y B G ELG	Y B G ELG
	Y B G ELG	Y B G ELG	Y B G ELG	Y B G ELG	Y B G ELG	Y B G ELG
	Y B G ELG	Y B G ELG	Y B G ELG	Y B G ELG	Y B G ELG	Y B G ELG
	Y B G ELG	Y B G ELG	Y B G ELG	Y B G ELG	Y B G ELG	Y B G ELG
	Y B G ELG	Y B G ELG	Y B G ELG	Y B G ELG	Y B G ELG	Y B G ELG
	Y B G ELG	Y B G ELG	Y B G ELG	Y B G ELG	Y B G ELG	Y B G ELG
	Y B G ELG	Y B G ELG	Y B G ELG	Y B G ELG	Y B G ELG	Y B G ELG
	Y B G ELG	Y B G ELG	Y B G ELG	Y B G ELG	Y B G ELG	Y B G ELG

Circle the relevant Stepping Stones (Y = Yellow; B = Blue; G = Green or ELG = Early Learning Goal) and write a positive comment as evidence of achievement.